S0-CUE-382

The United States

Alabama

Anne Welsbacher
ABDO & Daughters

Hatfield Elementary Library
Hatfield, Pa.

visit us at
www.abdopub.com

Published by Abdo & Daughters, 4940 Viking Drive, Suite 622, Edina, Minnesota 55435.
Copyright © 1998 by Abdo Consulting Group, Inc., Pentagon Tower, P.O. Box 36036,
Minneapolis, Minnesota 55435 USA. International copyrights reserved in all countries.
No part of this book may be reproduced in any form without written permission from the
publisher.

Printed in the United States.

Cover and Interior Photo credits: Peter Arnold, Inc., Archive Photos, Super Stock

Edited by Lori Kinstad Pupeza
Contributing editor Brooke Henderson
Special thanks to our Checkerboard Kids—Raymond Sherman, Gracie Hansen, Priscilla
Cáceres

All statistics taken from the 1990 census; The Rand McNally Discovery Atlas of The
United States. Other sources: America Online, Compton's Living Encyclopedia, 1997;
World Book Encyclopedia, 1990.

Library of Congress Cataloging-in-Publication Data

Welsbacher, Anne, 1955-
     Alabama / Anne Welsbacher.
     p. cm. -- (The United States)
     Includes index.
     Summary: Surveys the people, geography, and history of the Cotton State.
     ISBN 1-56239-851-2
     1. Alabama--Juvenile literature. [1. Alabama.] I. Title. II. Series: United States
(Series)
     F326.3.W45   1998
     976.1--dc21
                                                                97-3791
                                                                  CIP
                                                                  AC

Contents

Welcome to Alabama

Alabama is one of the southern states of the United States. Mountains reach across northern Alabama. The southern tip meets the warm waters of the Gulf of Mexico.

Many **Native Americans** lived in Alabama for a long time. Then French explorers came. Settlers brought slaves from Africa. Later, people fought for **civil rights**. That battle began in Alabama.

Alabama once was known for cotton. As Alabama grew, people started iron and steel factories. Many American space rockets were built in Alabama.

Opposite page: A fog-filled morning in the mountains of Alabama.

Fast Facts

ALABAMA

Capital
Montgomery (187,106 people)
Area
50,766 square miles
(131,483 sq km)
Population
4,062,608 people
Rank: 22nd
Statehood
December 14, 1819
(22nd state admitted)
Principal rivers
Alabama River,
Tombigbee River
Highest point
Cheaha Mountain; 2,405 feet
(733 m)
Largest city
Birmingham (265,968 people)
Motto
We dare defend our rights
Song
"Alabama"
Famous People
George Washington Carver,
Helen Keller, Hank Aaron

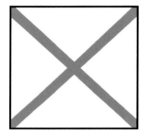

*S*tate Flag

*C*amellia

*Y*ellowhammer

*S*outhern Pine

About Alabama

The Yellowhammer State

Detail area

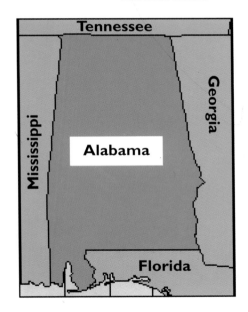

Alabama's abbreviation

Borders: west (Mississippi), north (Tennessee), east (Georgia), south (Florida, Gulf of Mexico)

Nature's Treasures

One hundred years ago, a lot of cotton grew on Alabama's rich land. After the **Civil War**, people mined iron ore, coal, and limestone.

Alabama is warm most of the year. The temperature is 90 degrees Fahrenheit (32 degrees C) or hotter during summer. In southern Alabama it is 60 degrees Fahrenheit (16 degrees C) in the winter!

Alabama has lots of water. Near the coast, along the Gulf of Mexico are swamps and **bayous**.

Hurricanes sometimes hit the gulf coast. Hurricanes are huge storms that are formed over oceans. They can knock down buildings. They can even hurt or kill people.

Alabama also has many rivers. The Alabama and Tombigbee are the longest. The Tennessee River is in northern Alabama. It flows north into the state of Tennessee and helps power huge **dams**.

Cotton grows well in Alabama.

Beginnings

The first **Alabamians** were the Paleo Nation who lived 9,000 years ago! From 800 to 1500 A.D. people lived in Alabama who built huge mounds. On top of the mounds were temples and other buildings. Then these people slowly disappeared.

In the 1600s, the Creek Nation lived in Alabama. Then came the Choctaw, Chickasaw, and Cherokee. When early Spanish explorers came to Alabama, many **Native Americans** fought them. Explorers brought diseases like **smallpox**, and passed them on to the Native Americans.

In 1619, the first ship of slaves was brought to the United States. In the late 1600s and 1700s, French explorers claimed Alabama. Later the French sold Alabama to the new United States.

In 1819, Alabama became a state. In the 1800s, battles grew between Native Americans and the United States. In the 1830s, the United States forced many **Native Americans** to move west. One move was called the Trail of Tears. About 4,000 Cherokees died of hunger or disease.

In 1861, Alabama **seceded** from the United States. Southern states wanted slavery. Northern states did not. This led to the **Civil War**. When the North won the Civil War, much in the South was gone.

Black people were no longer slaves. But they still did not have the same rights as white people.

In the 1950s and 1960s, the **Civil Rights** Movement began. People fought for equal rights for African Americans. Rosa Parks and Martin Luther King, Jr., were two of many people. In 1979, the first African-American mayor in Alabama was elected.

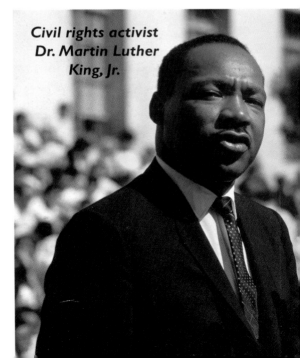

Civil rights activist Dr. Martin Luther King, Jr.

B.C. to 1500

The First Alabamians

 7000 B.C.: The Paleo Nation cross from Asia into America. They move across country and reach Alabama.

 800: **Native Americans** move into the area. They hunt and plant crops. They build huge mounds.

 1500s: The mound builders disappear. New people begin to arrive. First are the Creek. Early Spanish explorers are fought back by Creeks. The Spanish leave.

Alabama

B.C. to 1500

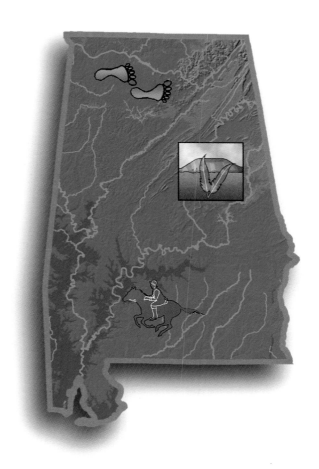

1600s to 1830s

Arrivals and Goodbyes

 1600s: The Choctaw, Chickasaw, and Cherokee arrive. The **Native Americans** begin to farm the land. The Spanish return, along with French settlers. Slaves from Africa arrive in ships. The slaves grow sugar and cotton.

 1803: France sells its land in Alabama to the United States.

 1813: The Creek have wars with the United States.

 1819: Alabama becomes the 22nd state.

 1830s: The United States Native Americans are moved to Oklahoma.

Alabama

1600s to 1830s

1861 to Present

Civil War to Civil Rights

 1861: Alabama **secedes** from the United States. The **Civil War** begins.

 1870s: The **reconstruction** period.

 1924: The Wilson **Dam** is built.

 1936: Jesse Owens wins four gold medals at the Olympics in Berlin, Germany.

 1950s: Rockets are built in Huntsville, "Rocket City, U.S.A."

 1964: Rosa Parks, in 1955, refuses to give up her seat on a bus to a white man. President Johnson signs the **Civil Rights** Act.

 1965: Martin Luther King, Jr., leads the Freedom March from Selma to Montgomery.

 1970: The first African Americans elected in the state since reconstruction.

Alabama
1861 to Present

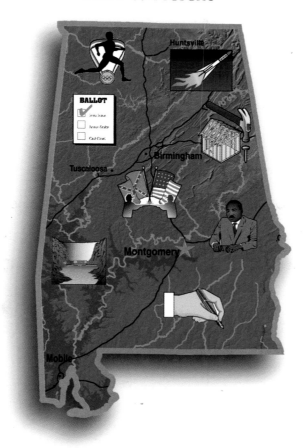

17

Alabama's People

There are more than four million people in Alabama. More than half of them live in cities. But many live in the country.

Many **Alabamians** are African American. Most are white. A few Alabamians are **Native Americans**, Asian Americans, and Latinos. Latino people come from Central America and South America.

Helen Keller was born in Alabama. She became a famous teacher and writer, despite being blind, deaf, and **mute**. Hugo Black, also from Alabama, was on the United States Supreme Court. Alabamian Harper Lee wrote the book *To Kill a Mockingbird*.

Hank Aaron was born in Mobile, Alabama. He broke the home run record set by Babe Ruth. Famous singer Nat "King" Cole was from Montgomery, Alabama.

George Wallace was governor of Alabama during the **Civil Rights** era. He ran for president of the United States. While governor, Wallace did not support equal rights for African Americans. Later he changed his views.

Harper Lee

Helen Keller

Hank Aaron

Splendid Cities

In the 1870s, two railroads were built in Alabama. At the place they crossed, the town of Birmingham was built. Today, Birmingham is the largest city in Alabama. The second largest city is Mobile. The third largest is Montgomery. Montgomery is the capital of Alabama.

Selma, Alabama, is 50 miles (80 km) from Montgomery. In 1965, Martin Luther King, Jr., led 25,000 people on a march from Selma to Montgomery. They marched for equal rights for African Americans. The march took five days!

Opposite page: The Alabama State Capitol is in Montgomery.

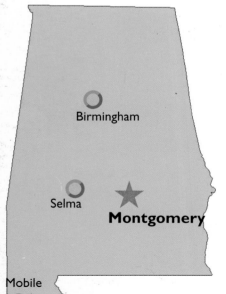

Birmingham

Selma

★ Montgomery

Mobile

Alabama's Land

The South has 13 states. Alabama is in the "deep south." That means it is one of the most southern states.

Tennessee is north of Alabama. Georgia is east. Florida and the Gulf of Mexico are south. And Mississippi is west.

The north part of Alabama has mountains. They are called the Appalachian Mountains. Below them is hilly land, called Piedmont. Piedmont is a French word that means "foot of the mountain."

The south part of Alabama is swampy. Much of Alabama has forests. Pine, oak, cedar, cypress, and poplar trees grow in the forests.

Alligators live in the swamps of Alabama. In the Gulf waters there are dolphins and whales. Beavers build **dams** in the rivers and **wetlands**.

The yellowhammer woodpecker is Alabama's state bird. Other birds in Alabama are bobwhites, quail, doves, and hawks.

Alligators and crocodiles live in Alabama's swampy land.

Alabama at Play

Alabamians love football. The University of Alabama football team is in Birmingham. There are many golf courses in Alabama. A lot of people visit the beaches on the Gulf of Mexico. The beaches there are sandy, sunny, and warm.

Each spring there is a Mardi Gras festival in Mobile. It is one of the largest in the United States. Also in spring the **Azalea** Trail is in bloom. Azaleas are pretty bushes covered with flowers. The trail is 25 miles (40 km) long!

People love to hear country music and blues music in Alabama. **Sacred Harp** music, a very old kind of music, is sung. Fiddles are played. Fiddle is another word for violin.

Every year there is a shrimp festival. There also are arts festivals and music festivals. There is even a peanut festival!

The George Washington Carver Museum has art by African Americans. There are many other art museums in Alabama.

Alabama has an **aviation** museum. The museum has one of the biggest collections of helicopters in the world! A helicopter is like an airplane. Its wings spin in a circle like a top.

Fiddle music is popular in Alabama.

Alabama at Work

Alabama has a large service **industry**. People from other places visit Alabama. **Alabamians** work to serve these **tourists**.

The **manufacturing** industry also creates jobs for people in Alabama. Alabamians make paper, wood products, clothing, and tires. Then they sell the products they make.

People fish in the Gulf of Mexico. There is mining for iron, coal, oil, and marble. And farmers grow soybeans and peanuts in Alabama.

In Huntsville, Alabama, there is a large rocket plant. Many of the American rockets that went into space were made there. Also, there is a space camp there for kids. In fact, there is so much space stuff in Huntsville that it is called Rocket City, U.S.A.!

Rocket City, U.S.A.

Fun Facts

•Alabama is called the Yellowhammer State. This is because Alabama men fighting in the **Civil War** put feathers from the yellowhammer bird in their caps. Alabama also is called the Cotton State and the Heart of Dixie.

•About 2,500 white **Alabamians** fought on the side of the North in the Civil War. About 10,000 African Americans living in Alabama fought for the North.

•Some islands in the Gulf of Mexico are part of Alabama. One is called Dauphin Island. It is 30 miles (48 km) long.

•The only lakes in Alabama were created by **dams**. The largest is Guntersville Lake. It is more than 100 miles (161 km) across!

•Alabama had the first electric trolley in the United States. It was in 1866 when the trolley first carried people through Montgomery.

•In Enterprise, Alabama, there is a statue in honor of a bug! The bug is called the boll weevil. The boll weevil killed many cotton crops. Alabama farmers had to grow other plants. This helped them find new ways to make money.

The boll weevil.

Glossary

Alabamians: people who live in Alabama.

Aviation: describes things that fly, like airplanes and helicopters.

Azalea: a kind of bush with flowers.

Bayou: a body of water like a lake. It is formed by rivers and oceans joining.

Civil rights: the rights of every person who lives in the United States.

Civil War: a war between groups in the same country. In the United States it was the North against the South.

Dam: a wall built to hold back water.

Hurricane: a huge storm formed over the ocean.

Industry: any kind of business.

Manufacturing: The process of making something.

Mute: not able to speak.

Native American: the first people that lived in America.

Reconstruction: a time in U.S. history following the Civil War. The North helped the South rebuild their houses, land, and jobs.

Sacred Harp: a very old kind of singing.

Secede: to break away.

Smallpox: a disease brought from Europe to America. It killed many Native Americans.

Tourists: people visiting a place, people on vacation.

Wetland: land that has much water in it.

Internet Sites

Alabama Information Sources
http://www.cptr.ua.edu/alabama.htm
Has links to news, business, education, history, recreation, weather, and general information.

V-Ten Online - Alabama's Premiere WWW Site
http://www.vten.com
V-Ten Online will help you uncover places and things about our state you won't find anywhere else. From big business to show business, we bring you freshly updated information, news, even monthly editorials about your favorite interests and activities.

These sites are subject to change. Go to your favorite search engine and type in Alabama for more sites.

PASS IT ON
Tell Others Something Special About Your State
To educate readers around the country, pass on interesting tips, places to see, history, and little unknown facts about the state you live in. We want to hear from you!
To get posted on ABDO & Daughters website E-mail us at "mystate@abdopub.com"

Index